Yellow Umbrella Books are published by Capstone Press
151 Good Counsel Drive, P.O. Box 669, Mankato, Minnesota 56002
http://www.capstone-press.com

1 2 3 4 5 6 07 06 05 04 03 02

Library of Congress Cataloging-in-Publication Data
Nayer, Judy.
    Adding it up at the zoo/by Judy Nayer.
    p. cm. —(Math)
    Includes index.
    Summary: Text and Photographs illustrate how addition can be used at the zoo.
    ISBN 0-7368-1278-4
    1. Addition—Juvenile literature. 2. Counting—Juvenile literature. 3. Zoo animals—Juvenile
literature. [1. Addition. 2. Counting. 3. Zoo animals.] I. Title II. Series.
QA115 .N29 2002
513.2'11—dc21   2001008001

Editorial Credits
Susan Evento, Managing Editor/Product Development; Elizabeth Jaffe, Senior Editor; Jannike
Hess, Designer; Kimberly Danger and Heidi Schoof, Photo Researchers

Photo Credits
Cover: Photri-Microstock; Title Page: Thomas Kitchin/Tom Stack & Assoc.; Page 2: Alan G.
Nelson/Root Resources; Page 3: Ted Rose/Unicorn Stock; Page 4: Erwin & Peggy Bauer/Bruce
Coleman; Page 5: Frank Krahmer/Bruce Coleman (top and bottom); Page 6: Ronald Cantor (left),
A. Gurmankin/Unicorn Stock (right); Page 7: Ernest A. Janes/Bruce Coleman (left and right);
Page 8: Halle Flygare Photos/Bruce Coleman (left), Tom Edwards/Visuals Unlimited (right); Page
9: M.P. Kahlm/Bruce Coleman (top), Frank Krahmer/Bruce Coleman (bottom); Page 10: Elizabeth
DeLaney; Page 11: Kenneth Fink/Bruce Coleman; Page 12: Roger Wilmshurst/Bruce Coleman;
Page 13: John Shaw/Bruce Coleman; Page 14: Alan G. Nelson/Root Resources (top left), Ted
Rose/Unicorn Stock (top right), Erwin & Peggy Bauer/Bruce Coleman (middle left), Frank
Krahmer/Bruce Coleman (top and bottom middle right), Ronald Cantor (bottom left), A.
Gurmankin/Unicorn Stock (bottom right); Page 15: Earnest A. Janes/Bruce Coleman (left and
right pigs), Halle Flygare Photos/Bruce Coleman (top goats), Tom Edwards/Visuals Unlimited
(bottom goats), Frank Krahmer/Bruce Coleman (top zebras), M.P. Kahlm/Bruce Coleman (bottom
zebras), Elizabeth DeLaney (left lions), Kenneth Fink/Bruce Coleman (right lions), Roger
Wilmshurst/Bruce Coleman (left puffins), John Shaw/Bruce Coleman (right puffins); Page 16:
Larry Mishkar/Picture Smith

Adding It Up
at the Zoo

By Judy Nayer

Consulting Editor: Gail Saunders-Smith, Ph.D.
Consultants: Claudine Jellison and Patricia Williams,
Reading Recovery Teachers
Content Consultant: Johanna Kaufman,
Math Learning/Resource Director of the Dalton School

Yellow Umbrella Books
an imprint of Capstone Press
Mankato, Minnesota

We see 1 eagle on a branch.
How many eagles do we see?
$1 + 0 = 1$
We see 1 eagle altogether!

We see 1 turtle swimming
and 1 baby turtle riding on top.
How many turtles do we see?
Add it up!
$1 + 1 = 2$
We see 2 turtles altogether!

3

We see 2 brown bear cubs
and 1 black bear cub
playing together.
How many bear cubs do we see?
Add it up!
2 + 1 = 3
We see 3 bear cubs altogether!

We see 2 seals on land
and 2 seals in the water.
How many seals do we see?
Add it up!

$2 + 2 = 4$

We see 4 seals altogether!

We see 3 giraffes sitting down and 2 giraffes standing up. How many giraffes do we see? Add it up!

3 + 2 = 5

We see 5 giraffes altogether!

We see 4 pigs in a box
and 2 pigs in a bucket.
How many pigs do we see?
Add it up!

4 + 2 = 6

We see 6 pigs altogether!

We see 4 goats on a rock
and 3 goats by a fence.
How many goats do we see?
Add it up!
4 + 3 = 7
We see 7 goats altogether!

We see 4 zebras drinking water
and 4 zebras in a field.
How many zebras do we see?
Add it up!
$4 + 4 = 8$
We see 8 zebras altogether!

We see 5 lions sleeping
and 4 lion cubs by a log.
How many lions do we see?

Add it up!

$5 + 4 = 9$

We see 9 lions altogether!

We see 5 puffins watching
and 5 penguins waddling.
How many birds do we see?

Add it up!

5 + 5 = 10

We see 10 birds altogether!

We see 1 eagle, 2 turtles,
3 bear cubs, 4 seals, 5 giraffes,

6 pigs, 7 goats, 8 zebras,
9 lions, and 10 birds...

at the zoo!

Words to Know/Index

Word Count: 330
Early-Intervention Level: 9